Alex Graham Bell

Written by Robyn Hardyman

Harcourt
Supplemental Publishers

Rigby • Steck-Vaughn

www.steck-vaughn.com

Contents

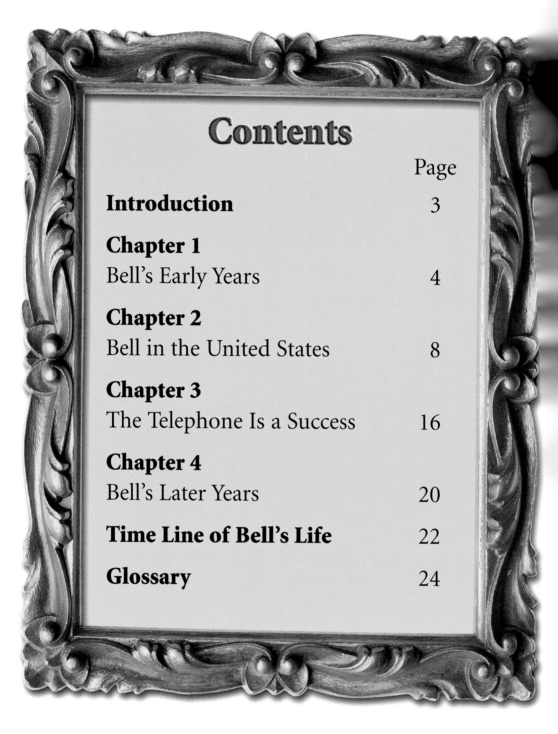

Introduction

Alexander Graham Bell was an inventor. He invented the telephone. Bell's telephone was a very important invention. Telephones bring people together. Today, we can pick up a telephone and talk to other people all over the world.

Bell speaking into an early telephone

① Bell's Early Years

Bell's Family

Alexander Graham Bell was born on March 3, 1847. He was born in Edinburgh, Scotland. He had one older brother and one younger brother.

Bell (left) with his parents and his two brothers

Bell's mother, Eliza, could not hear well. She was almost deaf. Sometimes she used sign language to communicate with other people. In sign language, people use their fingers and hands to form letters and words.

Bell's father, Alexander Melville Bell, worked to help deaf people. He helped them learn to speak. Young Bell was interested in his father's work and in how people make sounds.

Bell at age 18

Bell as a Young Man

When Bell finished high school, he went to live with his grandfather in London. He decided to become a teacher. He taught children with hearing problems how to speak.

Bell also began to work with electricity and sound. He wanted to know if electricity could be used to send speech sounds along wires.

Bell with his father and grandfather

By the time Bell was 23 years old, both of his brothers had fallen ill and died. Bell's father was afraid that Alexander would also get sick. He thought that the best thing to do was to move the family to Canada.

Bell as a young teacher

➋ Bell in the United States

Bell Moves to Boston

Bell stayed in Canada for only a short time. He soon moved to Boston, Massachusetts, in the United States. There he taught at a school for deaf people. He taught them how to speak. Bell taught very well. He showed the deaf people how to use their fingers to feel the sounds they made.

Bell (top left) with his students at the Boston School for the Deaf

While living in Boston, Bell read lots of science books. He also went to hear scientists talk about their work. Bell still wanted to find out how to send speech sounds along wires. He kept on working to find a way to do this.

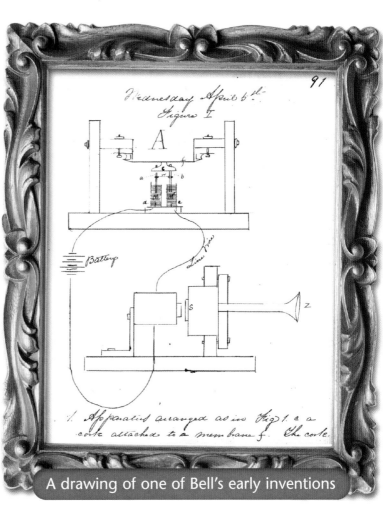

A drawing of one of Bell's early inventions

Inventing the Telephone

Bell needed help to work on his ideas about sound. He needed money and a helper. Two men, Gardiner Hubbard and Thomas Sanders, gave Bell some money. Bell also began to work with Thomas Watson, who knew a lot about electricity.

Thomas Watson

Bell and Watson worked well together on their important invention. They made a machine that used electricity to carry speech sounds along a wire. The machine was the first telephone.

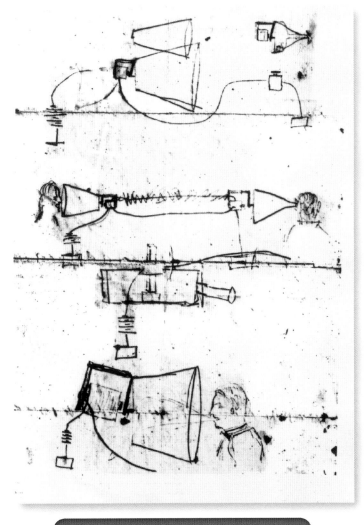

Bell's early ideas for the telephone

The First Telephone Call

Another inventor was also working on a machine that used electricity to carry speech sounds. His name was Elisha Gray. Both Bell and Gray tried to be the first to finish their invention, but Bell won the race.

Bell and Watson in the room where Bell made the first telephone call

On March 10, 1876, Alexander Graham Bell made the first telephone call ever. He spoke to Thomas Watson. Watson was in another room. Bell said, "Mr. Watson, come here. I want to see you."

Watson rushed into the room. He had heard Bell's voice over the wire! Both men were very excited. Bell and Watson did more work on their invention. It was important to make the sound of the voice on the telephone easy to hear.

Alexander Graham Bell and Thomas Watson

How the Telephone Works

Telephones have a receiver, a transmitter, an earpiece, and a mouthpiece. In Bell's first telephone, the earpiece was also the mouthpiece, and people spoke into this.

To communicate by telephone, people speak into the mouthpiece. The transmitter sends the speech sounds. Using electricity, a telephone line carries the speech sounds between telephones. The receiver gets the speech sounds. To hear a telephone call, people hold the earpiece to their ear.

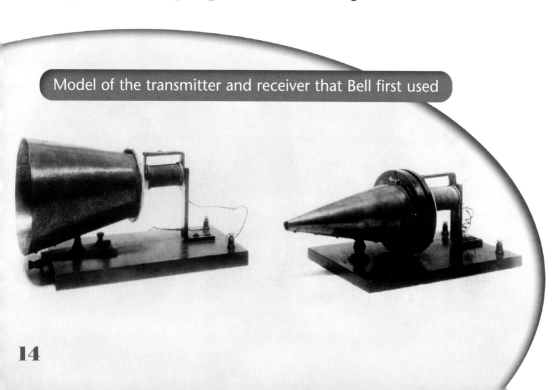

Model of the transmitter and receiver that Bell first used

The first telephones were large and heavy. They were made of wood and metal. Today, telephones are small, light, and easy to hold. They are usually made of plastic.

One of the first telephones, called box telephones

❸ The Telephone Is a Success

The Bell Telephone Company

Bell showed his invention to other scientists. They thought the invention was wonderful. They wanted to bring telephones to as many people as possible.

Bell and Watson formed the Bell Telephone Company. Hubbard and Sanders, the men who had given Bell some money to help him with his invention, also joined the Bell Telephone Company.

Bell showing people his telephone

Bell Marries Mabel Hubbard

Over time, Bell had fallen in love with Mabel Hubbard, Gardiner Hubbard's daughter. In 1877, Alexander and Mabel were married. They went to live in London for a year. Bell showed his telephone to England's Queen Victoria. She loved the new machine and wanted to put telephones in all her palaces.

Bell and Mabel Hubbard

The Telephone Line

The first telephone line was built in 1877 between Boston and Somerville, Massachusetts. A network of telephone lines grew quickly. By 1887, thousands of people in the United States had fallen in love with the telephone. The United States had more than 150,000 telephones, and England had about 26,000.

A telephone line between the east and west coasts of the United States was finished in 1915. Then it was time to see if the line worked. In New York City, Bell called Watson, who was in San Francisco. The line worked.

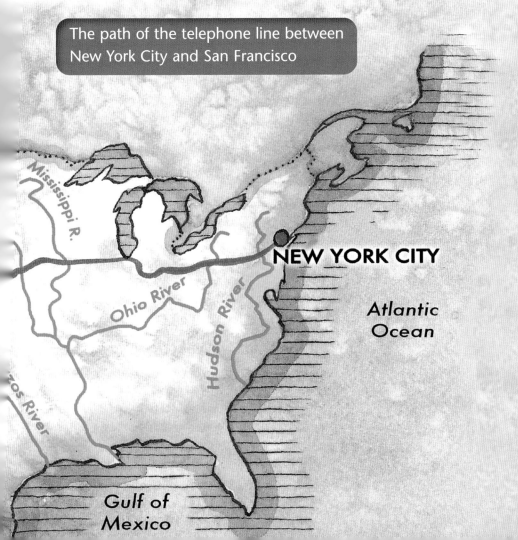

The path of the telephone line between New York City and San Francisco

Mississippi R.

Ohio River

Hudson River

os River

NEW YORK CITY

Atlantic Ocean

Gulf of Mexico

④ Bell's Later Years

A Lifetime of Inventions

Alexander Graham Bell's invention made him rich, but he wanted to invent more things. Bell went on to invent the photophone. He thought it was his best invention ever.

The photophone worked like a telephone. But instead of using electricity to carry sounds along wires, the photophone used light to carry sounds. On June 3, 1880, Bell sent the first telephone message on his new photophone.

Bell's photophone

In his later years, Bell left the Bell Telephone Company. He set up a place to work on his best ideas and invented many things. Bell made a new kind of kite that was light and strong. He and his team also built four airplanes. The best one was called the *Silver Dart*. It won an award.

Alexander Graham Bell died on August 2, 1922. To honor him, all the telephones in the United States were quiet for one minute.

The next time you hold a telephone to your ear, think of Alexander Graham Bell. Because of Bell, people near each other or far apart can talk to each other. The telephone brings together people from all over the world.

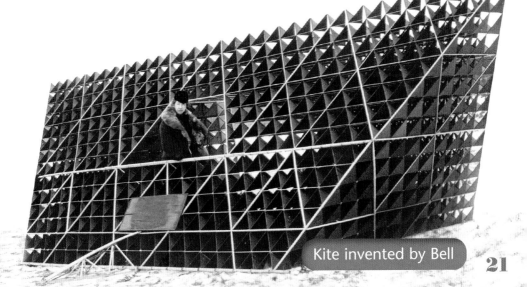

Kite invented by Bell

Time Line of Bell's Life

1847
Bell is born on March 3 in Edinburgh, Scotland.

1862
Bell begins teaching speech and music.

1874
Bell meets scientist Thomas Watson in Boston. They begin to work together.

1876
Bell and Watson hold the first telephone conversation ever.

1882
Bell becomes a United States citizen.

1907
Bell's light, strong kite flies for the first time.

1870
Bell and his parents move to Canada after both of his brothers die.

1871
Bell moves to Boston, Massachusetts. He begins teaching at the Boston School for the Deaf.

1877
Bell and Mabel Hubbard are married. The Bell Telephone Company is formed.

1880
Bell sends the first message on his photophone.

1909
The *Silver Dart* airplane flies for the first time.

1922
Bell dies on August 2 in Nova Scotia, Canada.

23

Glossary

communicate to exchange information, feelings, or thoughts

electricity a kind of energy produced by bits of matter that flow rapidly through a wire or other object

invention something made or thought of for the very first time

inventor a person who makes or thinks of something for the very first time

network a system or pattern of crossing wires

receiver the telephone part that receives an electric signal and converts it to sound

transmitter the telephone part that sends out electronic signals